TIL' GAY DO US PART

A.R.A

Illustrated by: ISABEL D.

TIL' GAY DO US PART

Book and Cover design by Norbert Elnar
Interior Design by Lance Butler, Concise Consulting Agency
ISBN: 978-1-948581-70-7

First Edition: April 2020

DEDICATION

I have dedicated this book to inspire and equip everyone in my world with the truth of true freedom and security. My heart is that all would see that anything is possible, especially those who struggled to see the hope in my journey. It is also dedicated to my family, the ones that always believed in my strength as I fought for my life. To my mother, who prayed furiously, and my father, for his wisdom and insight over the years. To my brother, for his protective heart. To my sister-in-law, and her love for my brother that speaks to me so deeply. To my older sister, for her constant encouragement and always reminding me I was stronger than I thought. To my brother in law, thank you for bringing a gentle presence into our lives. Lastly to my baby sister, you truly have made me proud over the years, how you have excelled in life brings much joy to me. To my friends, my high school girls, my camp friends, my college besties, and to my Impact Church family, you all have played a tremendous role in my healing. May you know I would have never gotten to the place that I am in without you. To my goddaughter and two nephews, you have brought so much joy to my life. I knew I could always count on you to put the biggest smile on my face. I pray that you all would grow up to be the men and women the Lord has called you to be. Keep shining my loves. Lastly, this book is dedicated to YOU! If you are reading this, chances are you are going through a tough place right now, or you have already done so. May you keep fighting! Do not forget you are worth it! You have got this! And if you are not reading because you have gone through a similar circumstance, my prayer is that you would use the lessons I've learned to bring you closer to the Father and strengthen your relationship with the Lord.

CONTENTS

FOREWARD

"Some people think God doesn't like to be troubled with our constant coming and asking. The way to trouble God is not to come at all." - Dwight L. Moody

The first word that pops into my mind when I think of A.R.A is "infectious". I met her in the Fall of 2007 during freshman college orientation. I distinctly remember the laugh I heard from across the lawn. Her laugh is one that will cover your soul with joy. She was someone that everyone on campus wanted to meet and befriend. God has blessed me with what I call a "sisterhood" that we have created over the past decade. When she asked me to write her foreword, I was humbled knowing how many other people she could have asked for this opportunity. These past ten years have been filled with joy and heartbreak, walking alongside her in this journey has been nothing short of a humbling privilege. I have seen her at her highest and lowest, and because of that, I have seen some of God's most significant work in her life and in those around her. What you will be seeing as you turn the pages will be a glimpse into her story. This memoir is raw, and it is real. I can promise you this; everything you are about to read is sincere and genuine. I was witness to many of her experiences. FaceTime allowed me to forgo that 300 miles were separating us as she was walking through the most difficult moments of our life. I could fill this foreward with pages and pages of memories that I have of how she was there for me even though she was hurting. We will save that for another time. I want you to experience what God has laid on her heart and mind to share. If you are hurting, in search of understanding, or simply trying to discover what it means to trust God, I ask you to read my best friend's writings. Her testimony is so relatable to what many of us women are facing or what friends and family members have faced. Let the words on her heart be a tool for your healing. I would be remiss to end this foreward without sharing with you the truths on my heart. Psalms 107: 28-30 reads, "Then they cried to the LORD in their trouble. And He brought them out of their distresses. He caused the storm to be still so that the waves of the sea were hushed. Then they were glad because they were quiet, so

He guided them to their desired haven." Anxiety, depression, and suicide are real. They are not a sign of weakness nor are they a lack of faith in who God is. Trauma brings responses that no one should have to manage, nor can they manage on their own. Our God is faithful to protect. I also believe that He has entrusted people to guide us in our recovery. If you are hurting, please contact 1-800-273-8255. This number is the National Suicide Prevention Hotline is available 24/7. Or you can find a teacher, a doctor, a therapist, your pastor, literally anyone that you can trust. He created His church to support one another in times of despair. It starts with one conversation. Please never forget, you are not alone.

AUTHOR'S NOTE

Growing up I always said I wanted to be a writer, just like my father and uncle. I only made the decision to pursue this dream when I finally got out of a marriage that left me damaged and searching for more of Christ. The purpose of this book is two fold, firstly, to give insight into the reality of marriage and secondly to show how God is a God of redemption and restoration. This book is to encourage those who have gone through a similar experience in their marriage, but also to encourage those who are currently going through a battle of any kind to fight until you've won, or in my case, fight until your spouse desires no more. I pray that this book would encourage you to continue to dig deeper into your faith with Christ, and importantly, to dig deeper into your marriage.

The Memoir of a half Ethiopian, half Southern Sudanese, Saudi born, Jesus Lover! Her struggles to overcome low self-esteem, and her deep faith that allowed her to walk away from a marriage that put her in the pit of severe depression and anxiety.

CHAPTER ONE:
THE BEGINNING

Growing up I was never the girl who dreamt of a fairytale wedding or even my "perfect" match. I grew up going with the flow, and as cheesy as it may sound, trusting the Lord for his perfect will in my life. I come from an amazing family; with happily married parents that showed the importance of Christ being the foundation in their marriage. I had such an incredible example in my life, however, it left me feeling I would never live up to their example. I grew up attending church from Sunday school through to the youth group and later attending a small Christian College. When I was in college friends all around me were dating, yet I felt as though I was in a different season and chose not to do the same. I remember being told I couldn't date until I was 18, which I never fought against and respected the rules set out for me. When I was a junior in high school, I was a part of a mission's trip that went to the Dominican Republic. There I met some of my greatest friends; Rebecca, Elizabeth, Joe, and Adam. Joe became my best friend, it wasn't until my freshman year of college that I felt as though I was starting to crush on him. My best friend turned into a crush that later evolved to be a boyfriend for almost two years. Without warning, he ended our relationship on Valentine's Day and left me heartbroken and angry. I chose to fight for him to find resolve, but in all honesty, I wish I had just walked away. I had gone through a tough season in life where I started finding release through drinking, something I never thought I would do, yet before I could find hope, I started to experience my first spouts of depression. I also had some great guy friends who I could have possibly dated but every time I had any sort of conversation leading up to dating, I would feel sick to my stomach and couldn't handle the idea of dating anyone other than Joe. I took a year off from dating or even thinking about dating and tried to get to a place with the Lord that I was happy with. I struggled big time. I couldn't find any joy in this time but kept holding on to Jesus during the unknown and trials that I was facing while in my deepest pit (or so I thought was my deepest pit.) After a year of not having communication with Joe, we ended up seeing each other at a youth retreat. The first sight I had of Joe left me overwhelmed. I fell apart, yet, it led me to a place of true surrender and a pure heart. The Spirit convicted my heart to remind me that I was not there to see Joe, but I was there to see students, invest in their lives and serve students whom I have had a deep passion for. After praying myself through the first day we ended up meeting and talking. We agreed it was time to talk and face the hardships that happened in the year we were broken up. We left our conversation with a decision to pray about our friendship. I remember coming home from this weekend retreat and the first thing I did was to see two of my good friends. It was as if they knew from day one that he wasn't the right one for me. They told me that I shouldn't be communicating with him, yet the stubborn woman I am bypassed any of their advice and continued. After three months of talking over the phone and texting, we both felt God was making it clear for us to date again. Throughout the divorce process I realized that at times we can become very clouded

17

by our own desires and in the end it can hinder our ability to really hear God. If I could encourage you one thing, please set aside your desires and wants and instead allow God to speak louder than your own wants. After some time of discussing our plans, Joe decided to start applying for jobs that allowed him to move closer to me. In the process of moving, he began communicating with my pastor at the time. In the three years of them building a relationship, Joe began to share some struggles he had gone through in his life which allowed our relationship to grow on a deeper level but also created some resistance within me. In the depth of my heart, I was worried about the negative repercussions that come with such pain, but deep within me I wanted to trust that he was finally in a good place, and I should have no fear. Now looking back at this, I can recognize that my low self-esteem hindered my perspective on the reality of this relationship being an unhealthy commitment.

Three years passed in our relationship where I mostly felt he was embarrassed to be with me in public, and physically he distanced himself to the point where he never wanted to kiss me. The dysfunction became my norm as I settled and allowed my self-esteem and worth to decrease. We continued our relationship into an engagement, which led to marriage. Little did I know I was marrying a man who didn't have the desire to be with me in any sexual capacity. Growing up I was taught "no sex before marriage" and it was something I held a personal strong conviction about. I guess that's part of the reason I was okay with him not pushing for physical intimacy. Therefore going into our marriage virgins and clueless was how we began our journey. My husband NEVER engaged in sexual intercourse with me due to what caused our marriage to end. He was in fact not attracted to me. I knew that it was not normal, and I knew it was appropriate for us to seek counsel, yet he refused. I made the decision to marry my best friend because I loved him, I wanted to see a future with him. I had hope for what God was going to do in our marriage through us. Our marriage was built on Christ, but when I began to fall into the depression of not being wanted, not feeling loved and feeling worthless, our marriage was no longer built on the Lord. Instead it evolved into me feeling as though I had a roommate and not a husband. It began to spiral downward into a self-centered pit of shame and confusion.

CHAPTER TWO:
DO NOT COMPROMISE
YOURSELF

When I got married, I realized that I had to let go of my old self, my life was now being intertwined with someone else's. I could no longer live this life for myself, my selfish desires needed to go out the window. Some choose to stay selfish and stubborn, and others, like myself, get so excited to begin a new journey in life that we get sucked into it completely. For me, marriage was a genuine commitment, there was not an option of divorce, I was fighting until the end no matter what. Is that how you were? I get it you are not alone! I'll be the first to raise my hand and say that was me. I wholeheartedly wanted to please my husband, I wanted to make things right when I could and be the best wife I could. Only about a year after moving back home after our divorce, did I realize the true effect that my broken marriage had on me. Physically, emotionally and spiritually. Physically I completely let myself go. I stopped going to the gym, I was gaining so much weight and didn't seem to care. I got to a place emotionally that I felt as though nothing was getting better. I felt as though I wasn't worth it and my body wasn't worth being taken care of. What a corrupt way of thinking friends! You matter! Our bodies are the Lord's temple.

For the same reasons, I was trying to fight for my marriage and honoring the Lord I also needed to fight for my body and honor my body as the Lords. Ouch! I get it! I always heard that growing up that my body is a temple, I just never really cared (to be honest). I just was like blah blah blah I hear that all the time is there anything else that anyone can say to make me believe that as truth? The powerful truth of what this scripture passage says has now enabled me to honor my body; "Or do you not know that your body is a temple of the Holy Spirit within you, whom you have from God? You are not your own." 1 Corinthians 6:19

As believers we are to reflect the Lord in all that we do and say, not in a legalistic way, we are all under grace and will never be perfect, but we have a responsibility to live differently. Only Jesus is perfect; I understand that I won't be able to fill his shoes, but I do know that I can try to embody him as best as I can. Why not take his word for what it says and make my body reflect the "good" work that He made? I know this may be a touchy topic, and hard to read, but don't let yourself go for ANYONE! You are worth more than that. You are designed for a specific purpose and your beauty that HE made will be cherished by someone one day. For now, do everything that you can to reflect him. I also believe not compromising ourselves is something we need to focus on when we are in the process of dating. I had the pleasure of getting to date after my divorce and learn what I was looking for. For such a long time in my marriage and even in life, in general, I felt as though I didn't have a voice. It wasn't until I ended a relationship, that wasn't even a bad one, but one I began to realize was not what God had intended for me, that I realized when God places desires in your heart for your future spouse and gifts that he wants to use in your future that you can't just silence those and remain stagnant in a relationship. I've always had the desire to serve in the church, adopt children, be able to host people in my home and allow my home to be a place of healing for many. I realized after dating for some time that I wasn't willing to compromise those desires that the Lord has placed in my life. Yes, it may sound like I am a stickler of some sort, but guys, I promise it's worth it. When you know what you want, be true to yourself and God- and do not allow any relationship to blind you into believing otherwise.

CHAPTER THREE: THE STRUGGLE IS REAL

I remember meeting up with a friend from church about six months into the marriage. At this stage of our marriage we were already having such a difficult time. I was so grateful to be a part of a new church; it was something my husband finally agreed to after many months of isolation. My friend told me I wasn't making enough sacrifices in my marriage nor was I submitting to my husband. I remember those words being said and deep down within me I just wanted to scream and tell her she had no idea of the pain I was in, the financial sacrifices, the mental and emotional, and physical sacrifices I was making. That was the last time I met her. I had no desire to sit with someone telling me I wasn't doing enough for my marriage when in all honesty I knew I was doing EVERYTHING I could. I was financially providing for our family, cleaning, cooking, and going to a church where I felt so alone and couldn't build relationships, all the while, not being taken care of in my marriage. Ladies and gentlemen, be sure you share your struggles, stick up for yourself speak up, no one else will be your voice. If you know you are doing all that you can, be sure that you make that clear. I sat and allowed her to speak words over my life that were untrue and detrimental to my mental health. I was already blaming myself for the past six months of a hard marriage and all that was going wrong, I didn't need anyone else adding to my pain. The lesson I learned here was the importance of being honest. Had I chosen to be fully vulnerable she may have given me different counsel. Be sure to seek wise counsel, and be sure, to be honest, and show your scars to people who you trust and want to be in your circle.

We are constantly told to always go to the Lord in prayer in all circumstances, which I never doubted and always agreed to do, but I had a husband who was not seeking Christ or counsel, instead, he ran to his family after EVERY fight we encountered. I was tired, worn-out, emotionally unstable, and physically unhealthy. It wasn't until a year and six months later that Joe decided it was FINALLY time to seek counsel. In his time of seeking counsel, he became nasty, distant and uninterested in spending quality time together. My marriage felt like a disaster, as if I was constantly walking on eggshells with him. It was a Monday, one I will never forget, in an outrageous fight he finally cracked and began to deflect his "miserable feelings" of the marriage on to me. He said he was done with God, done with me, and done with our marriage. He began to sleep in the guest room from that day onwards. I spent that week trying to talk things through, but he wasn't interested. Eventually, he left at the end of the week to go home to his parents. I was in a dark place and needed to be with people, thankfully my favorite couple from our new church opened their home up for me. In the 24hrs of being there I felt SO abandoned by my husband, it was dreadfully overwhelming and something I was certain I would never have to feel. My friends prayed with me and even helped me reach out to Joe. All those avenues were shut, he wouldn't communicate with me at ALL! Until my sweet friend decided to reach out to him and tell him he was breaking the covenant of marriage he vowed to me in front of God, our family, and friends. He agreed to text me and let me know he was going to be home later that evening.

That day I walked into our home to a man who did not even acknowledge my presence. It felt like it did when we first had broken up in college. My husband started the conversation off by discussing his feelings about church and how he had felt unengaged with individuals (which I couldn't sit and listen to because it was a complete lie). He and I were both extremely involved in our church and he was involved in a couple of different Bible studies. And then the frightening truth came out; he had been going to therapy and "figuring himself out" and realized that he was "living a lie" and could no longer live it. As a social worker, immediately I knew where this conversation was going when he said as he had been "figuring himself out." I began to put all the pieces together and asked him "what is the lie that you're living?" He was unable to muster the ability to utter the words. I looked at him once more and said: "what is the lie.... that you are gay?" He nodded his head yes. I was beside myself; no part of my heart was ready to handle what had just been thrown at me. I took a moment to process and then decided to ask the next question... "Wait; BI? Or GAY?" He looked at me as if I had ten heads and said, "gay." My final question came running out of my mouth; "so you're not attracted to me?" And as I heard him say the word "no" I physically felt as if someone had punched me in my gut. I couldn't believe my HUSBAND, the man who had vowed for better or for worse, would ever speak those words to my face. I called my family right away asking my mother if she loved me and my dad if he loved me. All I wanted to know is that someone still loved me and that they hadn't left my side. Thankfully my brother and sister-in-law rushed to be with me and picked me up from our apartment. I hopelessly sobbed as my brother wiped the tears from my eyes, and my sister-in-law compassionately held me reminding me of how much she loved me. My heart was so safe, I knew for certain that I was going to be taken care of. I finally got a full night's rest after a week of not eating well and not sleeping at all. It was then that I truly knew I had a family that loved me so much. Although I had lost my marriage before my very own eyes, I was comforted with love I didn't know ran so deep. I had a mother who was heartbroken and by my side, a father that was out of the country but intentionally told me he loved me, which was actually one of the first times I vividly remember him telling me he loved me through words and kindly said: "come home, my child." I was blessed with a sister who made sure to remind me that this heartache was not my fault, and a big brother and sister-in-law who came to my rescue and took me to safety.

Life brings two types of people our way, it is something that I learned quickly through the process of the divorce. Ones that we can trust forever, and ones that seem to be trusted in the beginning and then turn out to be someone we never knew. Sadly, it didn't take long for me to realize that my ex-husband wasn't ready to share the new life he lived, instead he spread harsh rumors about why things didn't work out. However, my sometimes-flustered heart knew that the truth sets one free, and the truth will always come to the light. I am beyond grateful to know that although my ex-husband had every desire to tarnish my name, I had my real friends knowing the truth and did not blink to believe those lies. Isn't that what Christ wants of us? Not to believe the lies of Satan. To be able to stand secure in the truth of who He has called us. Are there people that are beginning to tarnish your name, are there lies that are being spoken about your character? Rest assured, it's not just you! This is a common theme in divorce. Believe in who you know you are, who others know you as, but MOST importantly in who Christ says you are. **Psalm 17:1-2** states "Hear a just cause, O LORD; attend to my cry! Give ear to my prayer from lips free of deceit! From your presence let my vindication come! Let your eyes behold the right!"

I want to leave you with a few passages from scripture that speak to who Christ says you are. May these be the words that you lean on and the truths you allow to speak louder.

1 Peter 2:9 "But you are a chosen race, a royal priesthood, a holy nation, a people for his own possession, that you may proclaim the excellencies of him who called you out of darkness into his marvelous light."

Galatians 2:20 "I have been crucified with Christ. It is no longer I who live, but Christ who lives in me. And the life I now live in the flesh I live by faith in the Son of God, who loved me and gave himself for me."

Colossians 3:12 "Put on then, as God's chosen ones, holy and beloved, compassionate hearts, kindness, humility, meekness, and patience,"

2 Corinthians 5:20 "Therefore, we are ambassadors for Christ, God making his appeal through us. We implore you on behalf of Christ, be reconciled to God."

CHAPTER FOUR: FORGIVENESS BRINGS FREEDOM

Can we take some more time to be honest? Divorce is not a pretty thing. I have heard this said many times "no happy marriage ends in divorce." Isn't that true? I know when I first got married, even as tough as it was, we still went through a honeymoon phase where we enjoyed being together. Where we would go away and enjoy short trips as much as we could because we were "happy." When our marriage began to disintegrate, I was miserable yet with the fakest happy face I could put on. I perfected the "happy face." People were blown away by my skills of pretending for such a long time. I knew things weren't going to work out; it couldn't the way things were going. So, to give light to that quote, there is powerful truth to it. If we were truly happy, our marriage would have never ended.

When you go through the divorce process you see the true colors of the person you married. You think that you've seen the real them in your marriage, but I know I sure didn't. When I moved back home, I took nothing other than my crockpot, my laptop, and my clothes. He got to enjoy all the wedding gifts- all the furniture (that I paid for) and even a car that was fully under my name for almost a year. So much money was lost through our divorce and while I struggled to push back the opinions of friends saying I needed to fight for it, my heart knew it was better I walk away. As nice as it would have been to get all the money back, I realized how tired I was and had no desire to continue to fight more for something I wasn't guaranteed. The one peace I had was knowing what the Devil tried to steal and use for my downfall, the Lord was going to use for my elevation. You might ask how is this even possible? How can you be so sure? Guys, I knew I wasn't wrong in my stance; I knew I did the best I could when I was married and as I went through my divorce, and beyond that, I chose to trust Jesus. The Lord delights in simple obedience and He will honor my actions. Stay true to yourself; do not let the Devil steal your joy through your process. Come to a place of peace. You may ask how is it even possible to come to a place of peace? Well, I am glad you asked. I think simply submitting your fear or anxiety to God is the starting place. Speaking out what you are currently feeling to the Lord is key. The passage that comes to my mind is **1 Peter 5:7 "Casting all your anxieties on him, because he cares for you."** As it states clearly here He cares for you! He wants you to communicate with him how you are feeling. It's worth it. When you do, you will be able to forgive the wrongdoings of your ex. He or she is simply blinded by the lies they are living and are going to hold on to that deeply until the Lord begins to convict them. In the beginning, I shared with you the importance of building a community with genuine people who would never leave your side and then shared how I had many people walk away from me. As I went through my divorce this reality became a daily encounter and I was forced to deal with betrayal on so many levels. It was one of the toughest pills to swallow as I watched individuals walk away from me. A few months into my divorce and healing process, I found myself praying and releasing these individuals. It was hard, but I knew without a doubt that it would hurt me more than it would hurt them if I chose not to let it all go. Many times, I asked myself; "What I could have done differently, why is it that people that walked with me for many years of my life were walking away from me?" One of the individuals that played a HUGE role in my life yet I felt deeply hurt by throughout the divorce. A year and a half later, we decided to meet. I had no fear. I wanted to see her and not feel as though I had to sit in the corner in silence. Instead of going and bashing her about what was done wrong, I went in with grace knowing that God had already given me the ability to forgive her. Half of the battle of forgiveness and freedom happened on my own. By the time I saw her I knew I was able to fully release her. I walked in with a forgiving heart; I was able to see her with grace instead of rage. Isn't that freeing? Do you find yourself right now holding captive onto someone that has hurt you deeply? Take a minute to pray this with me and allow God to do the work of forgiveness on your heart.

"Dear Jesus, I come before you, thanking you for the individuals you have put into my life. There is no doubt I have been blessed. I know you placed these people in my life for seasons, and others for many years. Jesus my heart is aching right now at the loss of _____ (insert name) and I want to be in a place where we can laugh, cry and encourage each other again. Lord, I pray that in this time that I begin to process through the anger that I am holding onto, I release them into your arms. Lord forgiveness is part of your beautiful redemption story and I want to honor you and you alone. May these words coming from my mouth be pleasing to your ears. Jesus, I pray that from this day forward, I would no longer hold on to bitterness, and instead, hold on to grace. I trust that in your time things will be made right. I pray all this in your precious son's name. Amen."

If you prayed this prayer, my heart's desire is that you would hold on to hope and know that the individual who has hurt you or walked out on you, will return in the Lord's timing. His perfect timing, not yours. I can promise you, if I was able to find renewed hope and joy, you will too.

CHAPTER FIVE: RETURNING TO YOUR FIRST LOVE

The journey I went through in marriage led me to seek the Lord with all my being. I had the incredible blessing of running to Jesus despite EVERYTHING that I had going on. It was as if I was running away from the "earthly" man that I loved and back to my Abba Father, the one who was my FIRST love, the one who formed me in my mother's womb, the ONE who NEVER left me! I couldn't believe I had the blessing of doing that. The greatest love story of all time is that of Jesus coming to earth. Right from the beginning to the very end of His time on earth, He LOVED! I have had the blessing of being a recipient of that same love that Christ has so generously lavished on me.

Lessons learned throughout my divorce and beyond....

1. **God is our protector**

   As a believer, one of the character traits I have always identified the Lord with, is a protector. He is our Heavenly Father, and as a father, we see Him as our protector. It wasn't until I began to reflect on my marriage that I realized that the protection of the Lord was all over me. Isn't that way things usually are? Not until we go through a trial and come out the other end, do we see the lesson that has come from it. The Lord graciously and gently put His hands upon me so I wouldn't go through anything more miserable. Guys! Hear me out, His desire is to love you, and when you are loved by someone, they want to protect you. I pray that if you are feeling as though you are not heard, and that you can't see a reason for your storm, know above all else, He hasn't left you! He is right there, simply open yourself fully to Him. Be encouraged, allow this scripture to speak volumes to the truth of God being our protector and leaving us. Deuteronomy 31:6 states, "Be strong and courageous. Do not fear or be in dread of them, for it is the Lord your God who goes with you. He will not leave you or forsake you."

2. The Joy of the Lord is our strength

Joy has always been a part of who I am, right to my very core, in fact, it is the first word that people use to describe me. In my weakest moments, I found myself overflowing an insurmountable amount of joy. I could never explain it, other than knowing that it was the joy of the Lord within my deepest being. As I grieved the loss of my marriage and husband, I continued to cling onto Jesus. As time passed my true self began to reemerge, it felt like I was given a second breath of air. Simultaneously the Lord used me to bless those in my world as they found courage in my dependence and love for Jesus. Joy is no small thing, and now I can say, with true conviction, that there is immense power that comes with the joy of the Lord. It is yours to freely take. I remember how a new church friend shared she only ever saw joy when she saw me, she was clueless to my pain until we spoke over lunch. There is a joy that surpasses understanding and glorifies God. I will always hold this joy with honor and celebration; trials do NOT need to steal your joy. I can't help but praise God for all of this. There is no room for me to take credit. I know without a doubt that my joy flows in from my Father and I will be forever thankful. I pray that as you walk through your season of life that you would hang on to the joy that Lord has given you. May Satan nor anyone else on earth steal that from you. You serve a God who mourns with you but also rejoices with you. He takes delight in your moments of joy even in your weakness. **Nehemiah 8:10 "And do not be grieved, for the joy of the Lord is your strength."**

3. We are not meant to live our journey alone

I began to look for a new church in my new suburb. I chose to settle in a new church to embrace a new season with less recurring questions of my past and, just maybe, enjoy being lost in "the crowd" for a little. The first Sunday I decided to go I was embraced with the biggest hug. I was blown away; I couldn't understand why I was at a church that was embracing my brokenness so freely. Over this next season, I truly learned the power of the community. I was committed to surrounding myself with people who loved me and wanted to know me. Guys! It's true; we are not meant to live our Christian walks alone. We are adopted as His sons and daughters, which in the end also means that we've got brothers and sisters that we get to commune with. My prayer is that you would surround yourself with people that will speak life into your darkest places but also stand by you through your victories. Allow people to love you and encourage you, take you out to coffee, let them be the CHURCH that the Lord has called them to be. When I was thinking of ways to present examples of this, I couldn't think of a better way than sharing some pictures of messages that I received during my time of healing. Please allow people to speak these types of words over your life.

[_____] She is a constant friend. A prayer warrior. A worshipper. A joy-giver. A faithful listener. A voice of reason. She is available always. Smiling always. Hoping always. She exudes confidence, strength, beauty and wisdom. She learns from her mistakes. She rights her wrongs. She loves well. She is patient, kind, trustworthy and loyal. She is the kind of woman I want to surround, protect, shepherd and guard Farah in the crucial years, you know? Good thing she's a youth group leader 😊

[____] you are a gem in not only my life, but [____] and I am SO thankful that you choose us, that you choose her. I am so excited for the season you are entering into and can't wait to see what God does! [_____]

So your wedding song came on my play list and I was too lazy to change it but then the song "nothing is wasted" came on after. I got teary eyed thinking about your next love story. It's going to be the most beautiful one ever, full of redemption and Gods hand written all over it. I weirdly didn't cry at your wedding with▬▬ but I know I will be a crying mess at this next one. I know you're anxious with these next few days coming up but I know God has you.

Go ▬▬▬ The Lord calls you Strong and He is pleased in how you still cling to Him. Just like tonight when I spoke of tragedy, God used it to bring clarity and He will do the same for you and all that you have went through. Just like Ms. Maxine, God is reclaiming Your time!!! Go

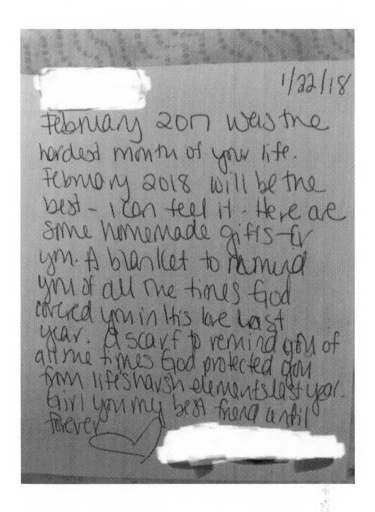

Do not surround yourself with people that are going to discourage you. When I think of my friends, the biggest thing that comes to mind is the amazing encouragement they have been in my life. From simple messages being sent, like those above, to lunches and dinners, some spent in tears and others in hysterical laughter.

My hope is that you would read these and be encouraged, and more than anything, begin to evaluate your friendship circle. Now, before you say you've tried, I want to acknowledge that there may be moments that you will try to get connected with individuals in church or other settings, and despite your grand efforts, you still seem to be alone. I certainly went through this and felt that as I began trying to build relationships that it wasn't as easy as I had hoped, even with people from church. It was tough, many of the people I had done life with for years were now far away from my new home. I had to start from scratch whether I wanted to or not. With my old mindset, I would have used it to look for another church, or even take time away from the church. I think that mindset was very destructive. Instead, I used this season to truly evaluate myself. I started to think of what areas I could improve on in terms of being more approachable and open. Rest assured, even during feelings of isolation, and not knowing where you belong, God is still available. He enjoys intimate time with His sons and daughters. Be sure to be using this time of "disconnectedness" to be present with the Lord. He has something very sweet He wants to remind you of. I would encourage you to remain friends with individuals from your past. Those people will be the ones who have walked through this journey of healing with you. If this is not possible, connect yourself with at least one person from your new church community. We all need at least one individual who knows us and is willing to invest, love and encourage us through the tough moments. I had two ladies who have done that for me in my process, and if it wasn't for them, I would have been lost in the crowd completely.

4. He makes all things new in his time

The summer I left my apartment I made the decision that I was living for God first and foremost, then myself, and IN that, it meant taking true care of myself. I took a trip to San Diego where I was poured into by my beautiful friend and her mother. During my time there I was in a place of sadness. I so badly wanted to be at the camp I had served at for almost 10 years. It was difficult watching all my friends post pictures, make memories and have a special time without me. I made the decision to take the lead instead of allowing social media to have control. Being off all my social media apps for the week was the best decision I could have made. I intentionally took time to pray that my pain would settle, and my joy would be renewed. God did exactly that, and instead of sorrow, I had joy and this verse in my mouth "For I'm going to do a brand-new thing. See, I have already begun! Don't you see it? I will make a road through the wilderness of the world for my people to go home and create rivers for them in the desert!" Isaiah 43:19 Ah- these words couldn't have come at a more perfect time. Isn't that just the way He ALWAYS works?

5. God answers the cries of our hearts

I was in a place in my life where I felt as though I wasn't being used to my full capacity. I could sense God had more for me. I had no idea where I could be used and what gifts God would use me for, but I knew I was ready and wanted to be firmly planted in my new church. Even before I went into marriage, I had the greatest desire to be a mother. Leaving my marriage, I had many friends falling pregnant, and as excited as I was for them, there was a part of me that ached with the recurring news. I often didn't know how to manage my feelings; I became frustrated with myself because I had always been one to rejoice with those who rejoice and mourn with those who mourn. In this season of my life, it was the complete opposite. It's funny how God works! He knows exactly where we are in our lives in those specific moments and seems to allow our friends to feel burdened by His love for his children. I learned what that truly meant the day I was asked to be the godmother to my best friend's daughter. Although she wasn't my daughter, I knew that God used that specific question to remind me that He knows my deepest desires. My heart frustrations began to lighten, and I was able to be joyous in being asked to be a godmother. I am thankful to serve a God who opens doors when others close. Always be on the lookout for what He is doing. Allow the Lord to stretch your mindset. When you allow Him, you will be blown away by the way your perspective changes.

6. Always be available

As a believer, growing up in the church, I was always taught to make myself available and allow God to use my skills in whatever capacity possible. I knew my journey with the Lord was special and that He had specifically given me a gift of sharing my journey to others, but I had no idea where it would lead. It wasn't until I began to start writing that God began to open doors for me to start sharing my story. I clearly remember the very first time I was asked to share, the rush of emotions flew wild but my spirit knew this was God edging me forward into something greater. The first time I shared was at our women's church Bible study. I immediately thought: "Me? Why me? There is absolutely nothing special about me."

Those words that were being expressed were nothing less than Satan's voice wanting to make me feel small. No less than two weeks later I was asked to share my story at our three church services. If that isn't God, I don't know who it is. My encouragement to you is to always allow God to use you. Do not put anyone or anything in the middle of what

TIL' GAY DO US PART

God has in store for you. Your story is special and deserves to be heard. It's when we make ourselves available and aren't ashamed of the story God has created for us, that we are moved and convicted to share. He has created great things for you, and as I mentioned before, your story is not meant to be kept to yourself, your story is meant to be heard. There is so much power that can come from us stepping out of the way and allowing God to do his work. After I shared my story of dealing with depression, anxiety and how the Lord brought me through my darkest season, I was approached by a few people about starting a group for divorcees. When I was going through the process of divorce, I remember how much I wanted to be in a group with others who were going through the same season or been through it. I realized that there wasn't enough support for those going through the grieving process and felt God nudge my heart to do something about it. I took some time to pray about it before going to my pastors and seeing what they would have to say about the idea of starting a group. My pastor responded "you are why our church exists, 1. You provide answers to questions that are being asked 2. You have passed the test- you have gone through the process and are now able to impact those with your story to bring them to their healing." I was blown away by my pastor's response. I had never felt so supported by a spiritual father before.

One weekend as I was traveling to see my goddaughter and her family, I found myself on a flight where we were stuck on the plane for two hours after landing. As frustrating as it was, having to spend two hours on a plane, badly wanting to be with my niece and nephew, there are always reasons and God knows what he is doing! I sat there and made use of my time by quietly working on my book. To my absolute surprise, the girl sitting next to me turns to me and says; "I really like what you are writing." She proceeded to share that she too was a born-again Christian. I was so pumped hearing that from her. We began to talk about her life and the things that God restored through such a broken past and family. She couldn't stop pointing back to Christ as the one who brought her and her family out of the pit. As I shared some of my journeys she was mesmerized. She ended our conversation in speaking life over my future and all God still had to unfold; it was a genuine blessing and something I will never forget. I am telling you guys, in everything that you do, be available - you never know who God is going to place in your path. We are being watched, not to sound creepy or anything. I say this because we need to be serious about our witnesses. Be careful not to let things slip you by. God will provide more opportunities for you to impact lives than you could ever count. My prayer is that you would step out of the way and let God use your story to be the headway of someone else's healing. You aren't going through your pain in vain. There is a beauty that comes from your pain. Make sure you are ready and listening to what the Father is trying to speak to you.

Father, I thank you that you have called me yours, and have called me for good. Lord, I pray that as I continue through my season of restoration that I would remove myself from getting in the way of your work. May you create in me a deep passion for your people, Lord use me to help others in their journey. I pray that You would fall fresh on me. I pray all this in Your precious son's name. -Amen-

7. **Prayer**

I've always sought the Lord in prayer, well so I thought, until I found myself in the process of my healing. I realized how detrimental a healthy prayer life really was. It wasn't just about a prayer of thanksgiving or seeking the Lord for direction, or prayer for others, it was more a time for me to seek Him for complete healing, and to allow Him to give me strength like no other. There were so many car rides with passionate prayer and worship while sobbing. It was such a beautiful place to be. In serving at our church we are encouraged to have a prayer partner. But I didn't just have one, I had many that I could count on and pray with. It was one of the most beautiful times of my life. Yes, we pray for closeness, and intimacy with our daddy God, but we also pray to seek healing from pain. We were committed to using prayer as a time to stop in His presence and bask in all that

He says that we are. When I was praying there were many times that I would be in complete silence, asking God to remind me of who I am. Some of the most powerful moments are being reminded of who we are in Christ. Especially reminding me that I am fearfully and wonderfully made, that I was knit in my mother's womb, I am a conqueror through Christ, a new creation, and a royal priesthood. Just to name a few of who Christ says I am.

If you are reading this and feel as though you have no idea what it means to be rooted in Christ, or even feel as though you don't know what it means to be a Christian, I want you to know, first and foremost, Christ died for you- He loves you! Yes, you! God sent his one and only son to take on the punishments of our sins so that we may have life. Sounds crazy I know. BUT this is the truth of the gospel. You may ask what must I do to receive His love? I am so glad you asked!

1. Confess with your mouth that Jesus is Lord

2. Confess that you are a sinner and ask for forgiveness of your

sins

3. Ask Him to come into your life and make you a new creation, and allow Him to be the Lord of your life.

These steps may sound so easy, but I want you to hear me out: becoming a believer is beautiful but know that at times it may not be easy. It is worth it though. Knowing that you have been saved from condemnation is the most beautiful gift. I pray that you would understand what it means to be established in Christ.

Knowing this truth gives us reason and strength to take our lives a step further. I don't know where in life you may be right now, but I am going to take a moment to remind you that prayer and knowing who you are in Christ is more than vital to your growth and healing. May you take time to bask in who Christ says you are.

1. **I am made new.**

"Therefore, if anyone is in Christ, he is a new creation. The old has passed away; behold, the new has come." 2 Corinthians 5:17

2. **I am loved**

"Do not fear, for I have redeemed you; I have summoned you by name; you are mine. When you pass through the waters, I will be with you; and when you pass through the rivers, they will not sweep over you. When you walk through the fire, you will not be burned; the flames will not set you ablaze." Isaiah 43:1-2

3. **I am fearfully and wonderfully made.**

"For you formed my inward parts; you knitted me together in my mother's womb. I praise you, for I am fearfully and wonderfully made." Psalm 139:13-14

4. **I have been made with plans from the Lord.**

"For I know the plans I have for you, declares the LORD plans for welfare and not for evil, to give you a future and a hope." Jeremiah 29:11

5. **You were created for community (genuine community).**

"I long to see you so that I may impart to you some spiritual gift to make you strong—that is, that you and I may be mutually encouraged by each other's faith." Romans 1:11-12

6. **Your divorce doesn't define you.**

For me, growing up in the church I always knew divorce wasn't Christ's plan, and in fact, He hates divorce; Malachi 2:16. When I was going through the process of divorce, I was ashamed and embarrassed. I didn't feel judgment from my family, however, I felt it from many people in my life that I would have considered close to me.

Please let me give you a piece of encouragement, just because you are going through a divorce it doesn't mean God can't use the lessons for your good! Ah, isn't that such a breath of fresh air? Ladies and gentlemen, you have been created for so much more. God can use the pain that you have gone through to usher you deeper into His presence, or even more so, to minister to those around you. Rest assured, your fight isn't in vain, you have some serious joy coming your way. Wait on Him He will make it all right in His time.

Let us pray together:

Father, thank You for loving me so deeply, thank You that you are using my pain for something so sweet. Lord, I pray that You would renew a desire to seek you in prayer. May my prayer life be strengthened again; I pray that when I do not know what to say, the Holy Spirit would intercede on my behalf and that my heart's cry would always be Jesus, Jesus, Jesus. May I find the time to seek friends who will be willing to be my prayer partners. May I be strengthened and encouraged by my church community! I pray all this in Your precious son's name. -Amen-

CHAPTER SIX: THE POWER OF VULNERABILITY

When you think of vulnerability, what comes to mind? Do you start to feel negative or positive feelings? I know for a while I would cringe and freak out at anyone who told me I needed to be more vulnerable. I have worked in counseling for a while where many of the conversations have led to the topic of vulnerability and the importance of it when sharing your struggles with other individuals. Yet I totally understand why we don't see vulnerability as a positive action, sometimes, or shall I say many of the times, when we have been open and shared our feelings and insecurities, we have gotten shut down. I get it, my ex-husband would always shut my feelings down. When I began dating again, I feared the idea of being vulnerable and expressing my feelings. I lived in fear of being judged, or just in general, not being heard. Trust me, I've been there! I feel your pain, but I've also had the pleasure of being vulnerable to individuals and not feeling wounded afterward. Finding a healthy middle ground is important and you will experience such freedom and strength. I am not asking you to go and share your life with everyone, but I am challenging you to think deep within yourself. Being vulnerable in your state could lead to a greater sense of healing.

In writing this I have realized how raw life is, and without vulnerability in life, I feel as though our journey as believers would remain stagnant. So, in thinking of ways that my story can be experienced in a deeper capacity, I have decided to share a couple of journal entries I had written during my marriage. I don't want you to think of this as a time for you to feel sad, but may this be a time of reflection of the goodness of the God that we serve, that He saw me in my distress and answered my constant cries in a deeper way than I could have ever imagined. My prayer is that you would allow these words, and cries, to usher you into the presence of the Lord.

11/2/16
Abba, daddy, father,
Thank you for being my provider. My lover,
thank you for loving me so deeply. Dear Lord,
then I could have ever imagined.
Today & everyday I continue to see myself
for individuals at church who have been
having the desire to get to know me,
Not as (3 will) but as Amara who
you have called me to be. It has been
the greatest blessing to me knowing I can
go to anyone in our church and know their
hearts are so genuine, Lord I pray that
I'd be able to have such an attitude
towards my brothers and sisters @
Seven Hills Lord I am so grateful for
Elissa and Corey, to be able to have
such sweet friends that we are
constantly living & growing with has
been so sweet. lord.
Lord I continue to pray for the
I married, the man who has not
won me love in the curiosity I've
I longing for. God my heart tugs

I need you to move deeply in
this marriage. I am always praying for
a breakthrough but nothing has happened
It has been 1 year and 6 months and
I still continue to think of what
I have done to be so annoyed or
ignored. It hurts God and I can't
continue down a path so broken.
Lord PLEASE do something now! Right
now, not later but now. I want
to really connect, I don't want to
always be thinking what if... I want
to be certain in this and really
know and believe and be shown he
loves me deeper than his selfishness.
God thank you for grace & because
of grace I was/am saved, I know he
reached my sin is, but b/c you want
me so deeply you showed, and constantly
show me grace- (Experience/Quiet time)

4/19/16
God I'm tired of living my life like
this. Why is it ok that I am
not being pursed the way I should
be. Why aren't I with someone
who takes care of all areas in
the marriage. why have you done
this to me. I've done nothing to
deserve to be treated like this.
There is only so much more I
can handle.
When will I ever be taken
care of sexually? why me.... why
can't he take this seriously-
why can't you take it seriously,
I am tired of being unwanted and
not pursued. I've done nothing but
fight for this, I know this can't
be fair so why have you done
this to me. Will you begin working
in this. I can't take it. 11 months
is long enough I shouldn't be
dealing with this.

4/17/16

Today marks 11 months that we have been married and still I have to be let down, and into believing I am not wanted, I am tired, tired and worn all I want is have the real genuine intimacy with my husband.

We have been talking about buying a house, adoption and all of these "big" plans and yet the one thing that remains constant is his refusal to be intimate. I am heart broken, today and yesterday I was hoping. I keep being let down. God I don't understand why this is okay. Why, you haven't moved? I just want to be loved fully with NO fear with out selfishness set aside! I don't want to live like that. I am tired of being let down... I am literally heart broken

I thought you wanted me to be with a man who loved me with his all, that would take care of me and purse me, so why is it that you haven't moved. I've done so much to take care of myself so I can look like someone that he'd like but there is nothing else I can do I've tried why can't he try, where is the effort in this marriage. You both have give me NO reason then to give up and hope.

As I sat and read through these journal entries, I realized how truly broken and in desperate need of a miracle from the Lord I was. Though the outcome of my marriage was not one the Lord would have ever wanted for me, I can stand here in complete peace knowing that there is life after divorce! If you find yourself in this place of complete desperation and unsure what else to do, please as I have stated before, seek counsel from your pastors, or other believers, or even a licensed counselor. The Christian journey isn't one that is meant to be lived alone. My prayer is that anyone struggling would take this to heart and bring them to the place of desiring counsel. I felt very alone throughout my marriage and the struggles I faced. In looking back, I genuinely wish I had chosen to get help.

An area I found myself having to be particularly vulnerable in was with weddings and babies. Ouch, oh my, was it a hard couple of years going to so many weddings and baby showers. I began to feel so inadequate, I felt as though I was nothing and had nothing good coming my way. That's the problem with society, we find ourselves comparing what we "don't" have to what others "do" have, and let me tell you, it can honestly get you down in the dumps. I know weddings, marriages, and babies are beautiful, they are worth celebrating through and through. All are true gifts from the Lord and I never want to take that joy away from anyone around me. Thankfully I didn't, I rejoiced with those around me, especially with my best friend who tried getting pregnant for four years. She is also the friend who asked me to be to the Godmother of their daughter. I know without a doubt, if I wasn't open and vulnerable with the right friends, I would not have had the strength to share joy and celebration. My vulnerability gave me strength, not weakness, and allowed me to be in a healthy place. My brother is one I adore and look up to deeply. When I found out that they were pregnant, not one negative thought came to my mind. I had been praying for the Lord to bring a child to them, and in His time, He did. For that, I was beyond grateful. But ladies and gentlemen, when we find ourselves comparing our life situations with others around us, we will begin to feel as though our lives haven't gone anywhere. BUT let me be the one to tell you the Devil is a liar. He knows your weaknesses, don't let him steal those moments where you can rejoice with those in their celebrations such as weddings and new babies. Instead, be real, share your feelings with at least one person, because that will help you tremendously in being able to really find that joy, deep, deep down in you! Are you struggling with the idea of having to be vulnerable? Are you worried that sharing too much of your story may cause judgment to be passed? I think that's always a fear each of us carries. My hope is that it is the complete opposite; that when you begin to be open about your struggles, that the Lord's blessings would flow in such an overwhelming way in your life. I promise, vulnerability may seem scary now, but there is something so powerful that comes with it. I have found this to be very true in my life. Without sharing with individuals in my church community, I wouldn't have been able to start a small group for divorced women. Walk in the favor of the Lord and He will guide you to places you never imagined.

Let us take a moment to pray over friendships:

Father, I come before you, desperately in need of your people in my life. Lord, I pray that you would bring individuals beside me as I walk through this season of pain. Lord, I pray that I wouldn't begin to isolate myself, but that I would begin to reach out to the sisters and brothers that You have placed in my life. Lord allow me to be vulnerable. If that brings discomfort, let it be. I want to be in a place where I do not need to worry about where I am in life. I pray that You would use my pain as a testimony and bring beauty out of it. I pray all this in Your precious son's name. -Amen-

CHAPTER SEVEN: YOU ARE AN ARTIFACT

You may have read this chapter title and thought: "what in the world does this even mean?" I am glad you asked! One afternoon while on vacation, I got to go and spend some time alone in the city- one of my favorite places to go when I have any free time. I was so thankful to have been able to take the afternoon to myself. I was excited to go and sit alone while writing my book. Instead, I found myself in two entirely different situations.

I was watching a man that was trying to get revived back to life by EMTs. This was such an eye-opening and heartbreaking experience as I watched all hope slip away fast. I noticed two women that were sitting crying, desperate to get more information but were unable to do so because of the fire department protecting the man's privacy.

It's moments like this that you realize how fragile life truly is. The experience took me back to my personal moments where I struggled to find a reason to live. I had moments where I had no desire to even hold onto life. Wow! I am thankful for the ways the Lord uses tough situations to bring out some of the deepest life lessons. For me the lesson here was never take life for granted. For a while I had struggled and wanted to take my own life at the mercy of my own hands, but there was a man that was so desperate for his life but at a blink of an eye for him could have ended. After the man was rushed away in the ambulance, I took time to pray for the women who called 911. I chose to encourage and speak life over them. I asked if they would be willing for me to pray for them, and without hesitation, they said yes. They were beyond appreciative of my willingness to stop everything and pray for them. As I stated previously: always make yourself available, you never know what God is going to do during a situation. Most of the time I find myself very quiet, but God used my voice and obedience that afternoon to bring peace during chaos. Man, God is SO neat! I had the privilege of working at one of the most excellent places I had ever worked. Where we were continuously being invested in and, one of my favorite things was, our CEO wanted to know who he had working for him. I had the privilege of getting to sit with my CEO one afternoon and I remember him saying; "You may be quiet, but your leadership is deadly." I valued that statement so much more than he would have known and it was exactly what I needed to hear. I want to be known as a leader; a leader that leads with excellence and doesn't demand to be heard, just to be followed. Quiet confidence is something I value and have chosen to lead in a manner that is appreciated, seen and acknowledged despite my decision not to be loud. How do you want people to know you? I want to be known not only as a leader but also as someone who shines the light of Christ.

The other encounter I found myself in, was sitting next to a girl who was enjoying reading a book. The title seemed intriguing, so we spent some time talking about what she was reading and whether she would recommend it or not. Before long we were talking about life. I felt as though I had known her for a while. We discussed what she had done over the summer and some of the recent projects she had been working on. I shared with her that I was in the process of trying to write a book. Her mouth dropped in amazement. We immediately started talking about the book and the journey I had been on.

She was baffled and couldn't be more thankful for my openness. The next words out of her mouth were: "you, you are an artifact." I was instantly confused, what on earth could she be trying to say? She continued speaking words of encouragement and life over me. She spoke about how we do not get to experience many individuals who are artifacts and that there was something so unique about me that she couldn't let the conversation end without encouraging me. What a truly random yet truly profound appointment. My heart was so encouraged yet all I set out to do was spend some time alone. There will be countless times that the Lord will send love and courage your way when you don't even know you need it. Your role is simply to live your life in a manner that people can speak to the depths of your soul. When we are open and willing to receive words from people, gateways into incredible self-reflection open. I know I was personally blown away by this young woman and the words she spoke over me. You may ask, "How I can be sure that I make myself available to allowing God to work through me?" I think it's as simple as being present, smiling, looking around you, greeting strangers, and taking time to be off your phone. I think these are simple habits that many don't realize can play a large role in someone else's world. When I think of the word artifact, I am reminded of beauty because often artifacts are created over time. So, when I say you are an artifact, I mean you are literally a prized possession of the heavenly Father and as He constantly is making you new, day by day, you are becoming something so beautiful. I pray that as you let these words sink you would begin to be reminded of the beauty that's deep within you.

Pray with me friend:

Father, thank you for the gift of life you have given me. Thank you for placing opportunities in my life, even when I try to bypass them. Jesus, I pray that You would use my words to uplift people everywhere I go. I pray that Your name would always be on my lips so that Your love would touch individuals that I encounter. Father, I pray that You would give me a special anointing to love and encourage individuals around me. I pray all this in Your son's name. Amen.

CHAPTER EIGHT:
THE CHURCHES
RESPONSE

Friends, sisters and brothers, let me start off by saying I am not a theologian of any sort nor have I attended seminary. Instead, I am writing this as an individual who has spent her past thirty years of life within the church setting. I have experienced church; the good, the bad and the ugly. I have seen church done well and I have seen church operate out of a place of brokenness. Throughout all these experiences, I am thankful for what I have seen because it has taught me the pros and the cons, of a healthy church community and lastly, most importantly, the act of grace. When thinking about how I would tackle this chapter, I felt led to share my thoughts and lessons learned as a woman who was married in the church, and now a single woman, and still in the church.

I truly believe marriage is beautiful and that it can be done right with the help of those around us. I have seen a significant emphasis being placed on married couples, which is great for sure because there is a need for that, especially for those going through a trying time within their marriages. But my heart will always extend further to shared focus and attention to other crucial areas such as the youth, children and single ministries. The body of

Christ is made of so many individuals, and we all deserve to feel as though we are valued. I think the passage that we all know that speaks of the importance of the body is as follows "I want you to think about how all this makes you more significant, not less. A body isn't just a single part blown up into something huge. It's all the different-but-similar parts arranged and functioning together. If the foot said, 'I'm not elegant like a hand, embellished with rings, I guess I don't belong to this body.' Would that make it so? If the ear said, 'I'm not beautiful like an eye limpid and expressive, I don't deserve a place on the head.' Would you want to remove it from the body? If the body was all eye, how could it hear? If all ear how could it smell? As it is, we see that God has carefully placed each part of the body right where he wanted it." 1 Corinthians 12:14-18.

I genuinely believe in the importance of this scripture. It summarizes exactly what I want the church to be reminded of when it comes to those who are single. In all honesty, I have found myself feeling left out in different capacities. Yes, I love seeing married couples investing in other marriages and spending time with other couples that are also married, but I think there is a need for there to be married individuals still being able to invest and encourage those who are single. The reality is, they once were in our boat as well. My heart breaks tremendously because I'm not the only one who has experienced this frustration.

Some of my most precious moments when I was married were when I was able to take a moment to love and speak life over those still single. I found it to be the greatest source of joy because I knew that those I was pouring into appreciated it and were thankful that they had not been forgotten. On the other side, I, unfortunately, haven't seen there to be an influx of support, encouragement or even resources for those who are single. I am not writing this as a cry for attention, but I am writing in this in hopes that if you are reading this and agree, that you'd find ways of seeking the assistance needed within your church as you walk through your season of singleness. I believe singleness can be significant and one of your greatest seasons as an adult, but it can be equally as much of a struggle. There are so many times we begin to question our identities and feel as though we are not adequate because we don't have a partner. I think those are the moments that we need to press on to trust that in our season of singleness God is preparing us to become the best partner to the one He has created for us. Some are called to a life of singleness, but those who are will know, just as those who are not. I have been blessed and gotten to be poured into by my pastors. They know it is not easy going through a divorce or even a breakup; they are all hard. Those within the church can uplift us with such grace and love. It can honestly be just as simple as a cup of coffee with a married individual sitting and hearing what you are going through and then having them speak into your life to remind you that your fight is worth the wait. I know it is, I promise you it will be!

On the other side of singleness is the importance of the church responding in love to those who have gone through or are going through a divorce. The reality is, divorce isn't easy on anyone. Most who have gone through a divorce are ashamed about it and hate that they had to go through it. So, the last thing we want is those around the church looking down upon us. I think the stigma of divorce, especially within the church, has such a harsh covering which breaks my heart. I believe that women and men who have been divorced can offer just as much to those within our church community as those who are still married. There is something profound and powerful when attention is taken off failure and onto redemption. Sharing testimonies of healing and wholeness glorifies God in the most extravagant way that it would be a shame to shy away from a broken story because it doesn't fit the perfect "marriage story". Are you feeling as though you have been forgotten or as though you don't belong? I want to encourage you to have a conversation with a pastor, a friend who is married, or any others within your church community. It takes courage to do so, however, I promise it will be worth it. You will find a new level of peace and acceptance entering your church community. You are made for a specific and glorious purpose, you are worth being poured into, you deserve it, just as much as marriages do. In these moments be sure that you are continuously praying and allowing your heart and spirit to be renewed and healed. As you walk through your season through prayer you are in turn not allowing the pain that you are have gone through to seep into the friendships that you have built and the church you attend. I believe that we all can recall countless times we are hurt and then view a situation as exclusive or malicious, when in fact it was our baggage causing us to see with a hindered perspective. If we aren't careful to live renewed, nothing our friends or church ever does will ever be enough.

CHAPTER NINE: YOUR STORY DOES NOT END HERE

As I had gone through all the stages of grief, I began to realize that it was only right for me to begin writing a list of qualities I desired in my next husband (I know, as crazy as it may sound). I realized the Lord had put such a DEEP desire in my heart to be a loving mother and wife to a husband who loves every part of my being. I began a list of these qualities and then decided it was only right to pray and read scripture, ask friends who were married for their input and then conclude my very own faith list.

Here are the qualities I am going to hold onto, and I hope that you would too:

1. Respectful.
2. Honorable.
3. Loves me (you) the way Christ loves the church.
4. Delights in my (your) beauty.
5. Pursues me (you) in a godly manner.
6. Grateful for the way the Lord made me (you).
7. Appreciates me (you) and the things I (you) do.
8. Sacrifices for me (you).

9. Takes leading me (you) spiritually seriously and leads me (you) towards and not away from God.

10. Confesses his sin and repents.

11. Learns the ways I (you) feel loved and love me (you) in those ways.

12. Has a heart for ministry as I do.

13. Desires to get to know my family and my culture.

Let's be honest, this list sounds out of this world; and honestly, unattainable. However, because I am a believer, I know that there is grace that is going to need to be shown. I am not on a mission to find a perfect man; there is no such thing, I believe only Jesus is perfect. Instead, I am on a mission to live knowing I am valuable and worth the effort in pursuing and, one day, pursuing a healthy marriage with. May you know your worth and know you are worth more than a man not treating you to the best of who God made you be. I am thankful that I have gotten to learn this through my season of brokenness. The Lord has far bigger plans for our lives than pain, I have become a testament to that. May you hold onto hope and onto Jesus, He is your ONE TRUE LOVE! The one you need to seek out daily, and in all honesty, even deeper when you are in moments of distress. I pray that this book has been an encouragement to you. If you read this and felt as though my life story is one that is close to yours, please do me a favor and seek counsel, seek assistance from your loved ones and church family, and if you don't have a church family, may this be a time for you to seek that out for yourself! The Lord has the most grace-filled extravagant plans for your life, and may these be the words you hold onto.

When I began to start dating after getting divorced, I was so weirded out by the process because Joe was the only one that I had been with. It's funny how each new season comes with its new set of tricks. Getting to know new guys, figuring out what I found interesting and what I really didn't enjoy, all of it, such a unique and special journey. Obviously, there is wisdom in this season, so make sure you allow those you trust to speak into your life, but getting to know someone without unrealistic expectations and a guarded heart, is something that can be fun and pure. I met this man the Lord placed into my life, and I truly believe it was for a great season! I had to stop overthinking things, be still and enjoy the process. It's crazy what God can do when we step out of the way and allow Him to do His work. Because of my past, I was jaded and so put off by any men from the church. I had fallen for a man who seemed to love Christ and be the greatest Christian in serving the church, yet as our marriage ended, I saw how false he had been. Unfortunately, it made me doubt my own judgments and caused me to second guess every other guy that came my way. But, let me tell you, when you know you've got a keeper, he will never second guess his decision, and instead, he will bring you to a place of feeling well worth the struggle. One of the lessons I learned through my season of dating, is when your parents have gone through the pain of watching their baby hurt emotionally, they begin to put up walls and are afraid to let you date. I realized that my parents invested just as much in my marriage through prayers, and finances and they had to go through their grieving stage for them to be okay with me dating again. You need to give your parents time as well! I know that sounds like such a foreign concept, but it's the truth. Our parents are the ones who are closest to us, after the Lord, and they are the ones that hurt when we hurt. Be gracious with them. While writing this book I went through two "May seventeenth"... which would have been my wedding anniversary. I had amazing friends that took me out and parents that acknowledged those days. Although I wasn't really affected by the memories of being married, I was affected by the date that I made a vow before God. On one of my anniversaries my dad sent me the most powerful message I have ever read from him. What was so special, as well as unusual, was that he allowed me to share it. I grew up in a home where we weren't vocal about our lives to the outside world. I thought this book would be a powerful platform for me to share it. May you read these words as if it were your own father writing to you.

"I send you this message to tell you there have been many May 17th's in history. Some were sweet, others bitter, but all were instructive. Somehow many lives that could have gone seriously astray, got redeemed on this day. Others went down as they did not have a rescue anchor. Your experience of this day kicked off on a journey on a path festooned with heavenly flowers. Everyone could have chosen that. Subsequently, it proved deceptive. You fell for it because we all could have done the same.

As God would have it, at the appointed date, Judas showed his fangs. You felt as if you were in Gethsemane awaiting crucifixion from which you thought you would not rise as did the Lord. You did rise, after all. Quickly, you realized you were perched on a pinnacle where the devil had taken you to face a grilling temptation. Thank God you defeated the father of lies. Not only did you refuse to genuflect to his charm, but you also made sure he had disappeared into the swine from which he came. You were saved.

You were able to retrace your steps from the pinnacle back to your folks among whom he hijacked you. You remained for a while dizzy, unable to connect with your folks, burdened by guilt you did not will for yourself. Now it is the time to cement your connections with us, your family. Realize our humble home is your base, heaven that will never turn hell on you. This is the garden you were born into till the devil stuck out its two tongues, speaking contradictions, saying yes and no at the same time. Now is the time you enjoyed life unencumbered by make-believe stories of life yonder.

Yes, there is a good life in this world, and you will find it now that your eyes have been filtered by the sordid experience you have undergone.

Someday you will land softly. Trust in God who pulled you out of the crushing teeth of that vice with mighty hands. He and only he will see your way through.

Avoid immediate attractions. Look deeper and higher. Remember, it is you who creates your own value be it rare or common, high or low, happy or miserable. Seek God's voice in all you do.

My daughter, I think a lot about you. Think, I say, but some would say, pray. What I am aware of is that it is your happiness I seek to protect with what arsenal I have. Some such arsenals would take the shape of anger, sometimes intense. Please pray and you will understand my soul, a father's soul. If I say I love you, it may register cheap. My love for you is a colorful involvement of a lifetime. Do not expect it to manifest in one form or content. It is love as God meant it to be, one to which no condition can be attached. I say this and God be my witness." -Dad-

These words may have been tough for you to read if you had a father that wasn't present in your life growing up and hasn't been to this point. My prayer for you is that you would seek a spiritual father, or even greater trust that we serve a God whose love is so much deeper than any earthly father's love. Every person, whether aware of it or not, compares their earthly father, or lack of an earthly father, to their understanding and relationship with God. This can be the biggest mistake, God cannot be compared to any father, He is so much more than any human can do justice. Even our earthly fathers fail us, yet our Heavenly Father will never fail! His promises are good and true and He wants to protect your life in all that He does.

My hope for you is that these words would resonate with you. May you know that your day of marriage is no longer a day for you to sit and be saddened over. Instead, rejoice, rejoice in knowing that God's plans are so much bigger than what you have gone through. May you take the time to sit, be still and trust that in this process all things are being made new.

May this be your prayer for your future....

"Abba Father, my provider, my constant one! I come before You in complete surrender to my future. So often I want to take things into my own hands, selfishly thinking that I can be the one to bring movement in my life, but I know these are prideful thoughts and ones that Satan delights in. Father, I come before You praying that my life would be one that brings honor and glory to You in all aspects, my relationships with friends, my family, my church involvement and my job. May the words that I speak reflect who You are. Lord, I pray that I would hunger and thirst for You daily and that You, Father, would be my one true Love. God, I pray that I would be content in my season of singleness. Lord, I pray that You would prepare me to be the wife that You have called me to be, to be the one who loves her husband deeply and desires to have a marriage that is fully set on You. Lord I pray for my future husband, whomever that may be, would You move in his life right now and prepare him to be the man You have called him to be. God, I pray that You would move in my life mightily and that anything that is of Satan would be removed from my life. May I be fully set on You, Christ. Father thank You for loving me so well, greater than any man, mother or earthly father would be able to. God, I pray these words would bring You honor and that You'd bring life to them. I pray all this in Your precious son's name."

Amen!

ABOUT THE AUTHOR

A.R.A was born in Saudi Arabia in 1988. She was born into a Christian home and the youngest of three children. When she was three and a half years old, her family made the move to the United States and landed in Boston, MA. There she attended an Arabic church with her family for almost twenty years. She grew up in Sunday School, youth group, and served with the youth group after graduating from high school. Throughout high school and middle school, she attended youth winter retreats, and summer camp hosted by her church's denomination.

After graduating from high school, she spent ten years serving on camp staff with the BCNE. She attended a small Christian college where she was involved with the Gospel Choir and traveled to Trinidad on Missions trips with fellow classmates. During her junior year of college, she was on staff with the BCNE and traveled to South Africa with a group of high school students. It was in college years when she found her deep passion for serving others and working with the least of these. After graduating with her bachelors, she pursued a master's in clinical social work. She spent two years interning with the Department of Children and families and upon graduating spent time working as an In-Home Family Therapist.

A few years after graduating with her masters she was married. It was then that she began to realize the true colors of depression and what her clients had been dealing with. As she faced and tackled depression she was able to overcome the deepest pit of despair she had ever endured. After getting a divorce she found herself attending Impact Church right outside of Boston. The teaching of the Word and the community that she got involved in, equipped her to receive full breakthrough and she was healed of her depression. After a year of attending Impact, she made the decision to seek out counsel and start a group for women who had gone through a divorce or were enduring a divorce. A.R.A has an incredible amount of joy and will do anything to help people during their pain find healing. Her joy for the Lord is apparent in all she does. She is determined to shine His glory and will not allow anyone or anything to steal the joy the Lord has bestowed her with.

YOU WERE MEANT FOR MORE

A.R.A felt as though she would never make it through the greatest trial she had ever been faced with. Her marriage had sucked the life out of her and left her isolated and heartbroken. She gave it her all until the day her ex-husband told her the truth behind the life he was living. That day was the day she felt alive again.

Are you battling in your marriage, divorced, or currently going through a divorce? Take some time to read through this book and dig deeper into the reality and truth of who God has called you to be.

RESOURCES AVAILABLE TO YOU

Moving forward, there are areas that need to be taken care of that you may have not been aware of. I wanted to provide these resources to you as you process through your next steps.

1. National Suicide Hotline Number 1-800-273-8255

2. https://suicidepreventionlifeline.org

3. https://www.faithfulcounseling.com

4. National Domestic Violence Hotline 1-800-799-7233

5. https://www.psychologytoday.com/us.

Made in the USA
Middletown, DE
12 July 2020